ACTS OF SPEECH

Kaye Boesme

Aigletos Press
New Haven, Connecticut
2020

eBook ISBN 978-1-7357406-0-7
Print ISBN 978-1-7357406-1-4

Library of Congress Control Number: 2020918949

Copyright © 2020 by Kaye Boesme. All rights reserved.

This book was published by the author under Aigletos Press. Contact information is available at kayeboesme.com

The cover art and section illustrations were created for *Acts of Speech* by L. T. Williams and are copyright © 2020 by the artist. The artist's contact information is available at graytiger.net.

To the Gods

To my Daimon

To Friends and Family

To my Partner

To the Past, Present, and Future

TABLE OF CONTENTS

PREFACE .... **V**

PART I **1**

   A PRAYER FOR BEGINNINGS 2
   MISSISSIPPI APOLLO 3
   TO THE MOUSAI AT TAUGHANNOCK FALLS 5
   TO NYX 6
   IRON-MAKER 8
   PANDORA: AN AFTERTHOUGHT 10
   KORE AND PLOUTON 12
   TO HYGEIA 13
   TO ASKLEPIOS 14
   TO ASKLEPIOS II 16
   THE BIRTH OF THE ERINYES 18
   TO GE 20
   THE SUPPLIANT 21
   FOR APOLLON'S CIRCLE 23
   A PRAYER FOR ROUGH SEAS AND STALLED PROJECTS 25
   FOR THE MOUSAI 27
      I. Ourania *27*
      II. Erato *28*
      III. Kleio *28*
      IV. Melpomene *29*
      V. Terpsikhore *30*
      VI. Polymnia *32*
      VII. Euterpe *33*
      VIII. Thalia *33*
      IX. Kalliope *34*
   TO APOLLON MOIRAGETES 36
   TO THE ERINYES, WHO REMEMBER ALL 37
   TO MNEMOSYNE 38
   HERA 40
   ERINYES 41
   TO ERIS 43
   TO HORKOS 45
   TO HERMES 46

- CDM 47
- TO HERMES 49
- A PRAYER FOR ENDINGS 51

PART II 54

- A DAILY PRAYER 55
- FOR DIONYSOS 56
- FOR APOLLON 57
- TO ZEUS WHO RELEASES THE RAIN 58
- EXACTERS OF JUSTICE 59
- FIVE POEMS FOR ATHENE 60
  - *I. To Athene* *60*
  - *II. Thoughts on Deacy's Athena* *61*
  - *III. Three* *62*
  - *IV. To the Foresightful, Inventive One* *63*
  - *V. To Athene Mekhanitis* *64*
- NINEDAY 67
- THE NAMES OF GODS 69
- GE ADORNS THE SUNS WITH RINGS 71
- FOR MNEMOSYNE 72
- FOR COSMIC ARTEMIS 74
- FOR APOLLON WITHOUT MEASURE 76
- MIRROR 77
- LIGHT-SCATTERED FIRE UPON US 80
- TO APOLLON OF THE STEEP CLIFFS 82
- PLASMA VEILS 84
- WHAT IMAGES WE MAKE 85
- FOR MNEMOSYNE THE WAYFINDER 86
- TO RULE: A MEDITATION ON THE CHOICE OF PARIS 88
- REFLECTIONS AS THE WORLD FALLS APART 89
- △ 91
- TO THE HORAI 93
- EPHEMERALITY — JUSTICE — LOVE 95
  - *I. Ephemerality* *95*
  - *II. Justice* *95*
  - *III. Love* *96*
- ONLINE AGORAE 98

Concord, Faith, Harmony	100
PART III	**104**
Acts of Speech	105
Like Cassandra	106
The Cosmos — Void — Night — Radiance	107
I. The Cosmos	*107*
II. Void	*108*
III. Night	*109*
IV. Radiance	*110*
Like a Knife's Edge	112
Solstice Dawn	114
Hello, Iris	115
A Catalog of Doubts	117
On a Bench in College	119
Hermes, Giver of Joy	120
To Keep the Lantern Burning (Reliance)	121
A Gift of Ink and Water	123
Mousai	126
Rediscovery	127
Fragments With No Homes	128
Julian's Ghost	130
Inspiraling	133
Eumenideia	134
To Womanly Herakles	135
On Mysteries and Bonds	138
Enthrallment	139
House of Ink	141
On Thargelia	142
Suspension	144
ABOUT THE AUTHOR	**147**

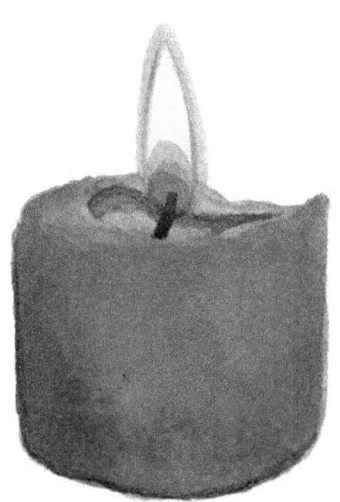

PREFACE

The volume of poetry that you hold started as a desire to have poems that I commonly use during ritual in a bound format.

For a long time, I questioned why I would bind my devotional poems into a book. They were, after all, functional — simple offerings, often rough around the edges, given out of duty to and love for the Gods. On entering my thirties, I had many loose pages tipped within the pages of sacred books beneath my household shrine. Other small papers mingled with stray spears of rosemary leaves and fragments of incense in my ritual supply boxes. It was chaotic.

In March 2019, I finally decided that I would do something with these — surely these poems could be useful to people beyond me?

Moreover, what about the poems I have *not* shared on my blog or printed, those that are not devotional, but that are still religious? The verse fragments? The personal devotional poems that I use to decompress after contemplation and good ritual?

As the project grew, new poems emerged, and unity coalesced. Things changed, as happens in life — in my case, getting deeper into Platonism, then having life change significantly due to the COVID-19 pandemic. The result is the volume that you hold.

Acts of Speech blends the public and private, the formal and informal. What links these poems is their religious context, symbolized by the act of giving offerings, a type of speech that was officially forbidden in the Late Roman

Empire (with varying degrees of success) when the Christian rulers outlawed household and public polytheistic worship.

It is also a play on womanhood and on women's speech, specifically the tension between remaining silent and being vocal. While women's rights have improved dramatically over the past fifty years, research studies show that women are still penalized for speech in ways that others are not. The rules of engagement often seem dizzyingly mercurial, with swift consequences for women who do not adhere to these norms.

In its first draft, this chapbook contained two sections — one of private speech, one of public. As I edited the poems, I discovered a third place, *performance*. In private, thoughts can be unbound — we have space to reflect and develop our own opinions and outlook. In public, we experience haphazard and formal encounters ranging from the familiar to the uncomfortable.

Performance is both public and private. The body is on stage; the words are published or recited for an audience. It is a *controlled* public. Psychologically, one is prepared for attention in ways one is not when having a flustered encounter stopped at a pedestrian light or answering the door.

Finally, the symbolism of starting in the performative and ending in the private is a way of marking layers of identity and expression.

Part I consists of poems that I have published previously elsewhere, along with others that read like they are being delivered to an audience. These poems are arguably *very* formulaic, created and curated just as much as any image of ourselves we intend to share broadly.

Part II treats informal public spaces. It begins with Hermes, who operates in liminal spaces and in the agora. This section includes fresh experimentation and a few semi-traditional poems.

Part III focuses on acts within private spaces, but also processes of identity formation, growing up, and the private sphere. It begins with incense and ends with Apollon.

We are fast losing truly private spaces, our havens of reflection and integration. It is in the quiet places where people grapple with difficult social questions that take time to understand. It is there where we process what happens in public, evaluating and constructing our personal narratives like spirals leading towards or away from unity, and where we can truly grow into ourselves without judgment. I wrote the first several drafts of this introduction before COVID-19 forced our living rooms to become offices, classrooms, and social spaces — before most of our lives became an endless cycle of video meetings — and these changes within the domestic sphere make what privacy we can still cling to even more urgent.

PART I

The God sits perched on
that pear tree, dangling sandals.
Carefree, he watches
your quick-darting hands
pluck the bowing branches' jewels.

A Prayer for Beginnings

2020.

First, I pray   for pure prosody:
Apollon draws   cool fire
from you, Zeus   beyond heaven,
ribboning truth,   giving oracles,
chords ablaze,   the beacon of harmony.
He gives all   their rhythmic skill,
pattern shining   like light within.
May it fill me up   like sticky honey.

Now, I pray   for sound beginnings,
father of the Mousai   filled with measure,
whose hands join tight   as they count their time,
their instruments copious,   their chorister one.

Next, I pray   for agile ways through,
father of Hermes,   the errant wordsmith
whose sandals fall   featherlike upon Earth,
who flies fast,   whom we follow fleetingly.

Last, I pray for   tact and strategy,
swallower of Metis,   bearer of Athene:
She weaves,   and in well-thought words,
calm wisdom finds its harbor.

Zeus, listen   to this petition,
provide me success   as I plan and labor,
completing work,   cultivating skill.
May you and yours   yoke our yearnings,
limiting boundlessness,   lavishing consonance,
our hands and minds   readying fast,
like light-scattered   fire within.

Mississippi Apollo

This poem was originally published in Eternal Haunted Summer *and later appeared in a devotional anthology for Apollon,* With Lyre and Bow: A Devotional in Honor of Apollo, *ed. Jennifer Lawrence and Rebecca Buchanan, from the publisher Bibliotheca Alexandrina.*

When you finish with that quiver and bow,
Far-Shooter, come to my wide arms, ride
tributaries to my core like a man tracing
his lover's wrist-veins with warm fingers.
Raise dams of civilization on my banks,
cover these curves with rock. Press your
domain up as far as you can: we parent
civilization here together, you and I,
Father and Mother, civilized and wild.
You walk among the mounds of one hazy
history, tantalizing meticulous seekers,
dangling flint and ancient burned bones —
that culture feasted us, too, back then.
Lay that bow down gently on my banks,
pass those shining hands over my murky
waters until mud sinks and diseases die.
Oracles come and talk gene therapy,
major and minor scales, conservation,
big-time developments: all worship me.
Variable, fickle — you teach them to call me
names when my belly swells and deposits
fertile mud over commercial farmland,
provide them with courage to toil and fight
rising stages, leaching earthen barriers.

Rages like these come and go so quickly.
Above all, when you lay down that quiver,
sit beside me and teach the tortoise to sing.

To the Mousai at Taughannock Falls

This poem was originally published in Eternal Haunted Summer's *Autumn 2010 issue, and it later appeared in a devotional anthology for the Mousai,* Seasons of Grace: A Devotional in Honor of the Muses, the Charites, and the Horae, *ed. Rebecca Buchanan, from the publisher Bibliotheca Alexandrina.*

We are far from Helicon here: great vines
feast on weather-worn rocks and climb gorge trees
cascading down crevices glaciers carved.
Once, Thundering Zeus freed his lightning smiths.
The Gods made this place a battleground; Earth
screamed and heaved beneath their massive armies.
You came only after the land knitted
itself together, cloaked by the new moon.
By deep pools where nymphai tie their long hair,
you slept: trees dropped their summer leaves and our
river God quieted the falls, misting
the dark sky to soften summer's hot night.
Fly once more to the dance groves far from old
hillsides where Hesiod saw your faces.
Here, we have always remembered fresh milk,
amber honey, and the pleasures of song;
our meadows flourish with infant grasses.
Hail to you, daughters of Zeus and lovely
Mnemosyne of the silent lake,
and remember always our Ithaca.

To Nyx

2020.

Nyx who brings the veil
coiled around you like incense
rising up to greet a starless sky

Goddess revolving
first queen whose diadem weighs
your head down down down I pray to you

venerable one
who coupled with Erebos
yielding Aither Hemera their day

untiring brightness
so strong it becomes shadow
the bitter Erinyes the calm Fates

the spirits of dreams
flying fast and out bringing
images symbols like messengers

Nyx of oracles
they were the first to give out
signs woven woven woven witnessed yet won

your stern attention
stills even Zeus when he looks
as if lightning has struck in darkness

Goddess of expanse
contraction the place that mutes
the tongue as if even stars sway hushed

accept this prayer
give success harmonious
as summer nights when starlight deepens

as if we too look
taking all advice within
you like a shroud revealing its truth

IRON-MAKER

Previously published in Eternal Haunted Summer*'s Summer 2010 issue.*

Iron stops all things:
fairies and gnomes,
highwaymen and redcoats,
terrorists and soldiers —
but most of all stars
blanketing the wide heavens.
Hesiod never knew all things
come from iron, so he placed it
after the heroes who pounded
bronze pathways to Elysium.
Without iron, primordial
stars would not have faltered,
gravitational equilibrium undone,
long before we came — or so some say.
Before Prometheus stole fire,
he coaxed iron out from bulging
stars' hot cores, keeping the balance
until the poisonous metal won.
The resultant explosions rocked Heaven.
Ever since, life has bloomed and withered
on millions of sun-kissed worlds.
Fires have burned on hot savanna
nights and in rainforest havens.
All the while, iron multiplies.
One day, it will smother all light,
even cosmic pinballs chancing
on voiceless singularities.

Prometheus waits there,
contemplating cosmic rebirth
in black holes and neutron stars,
decaying protons and newborn photons,
brown dwarfs and cold planets.
The Moira beside him takes forged
scissors in her withered hands,
running her fingers across numberless
seconds the universe has owned.
Under his watch, she snips.
Iron stops all things.

Pandora: An Afterthought

Previously published in Goblin Fruit's *Summer 2011 issue.*

You dug deep into plant-rich soil,
ripping up strong apple saplings
until you reached Earth's bones.
When beaten, they yielded marrow
more precious than fire and ice.

For my conch necklaces, you traded
amber pendants and silver thread.
I watched you build cities of gold,
burning the hide hut where our child
first cried and clay figurines rested.

When once we had nothing to hide,
jealousy made subtle furies of us all.
In forges, you wrought copper blades
for enemies' throats; on mountains,
ash altars to catch sacrificial blood.

What did you prove on that morning,
pouring dirt-covered stones into my
eager, accepting hands? What beauty
could I have imagined but shy bone
flutes and murmuring conch shells?

The painted dowry jar in my arms
tantalized you, a mystery you never
mastered, gained only through me.
Our son will say it carried plagues,

grandchildren that it concealed pain.

Someday, they will blame sky Gods:
I bewitched you through their graces;
my created body was ruin to mankind.
Truthfully, you never noticed my face
until I stole rawhide to bind my hair.

KORE AND PLOUTON

n.d.

These are the mysteries of life:
it metamorphoses constantly,
passing from generation to generation.
You will never see the same flowers twice.

Down in the darkness, sunlight will never
fade that wreath tangled in your dark hair.
I will crown you Queen in the crackling
darkness beside the lake of memory.

Once past the Stygian gates, time means
nothing but dust and echoes of lives.
We will see eternity in the blackness
and press against the beginning of time.

But if you prefer, stay with your mother
who smells like barley and amaranth
in the sun-drenched illusion above
and leave the mystery to another girl.

To Hygeia

2020.

How to praise you, finest Hygeia,
Goddess who bears the cup granting health,
whose serpent twists up to quench its thirst?
Granddaughter of Paian, preventer,
sanitation engineers give their thanks,
virologists release new vaccines,
and the many flourish under you.
Your dance is the rhythm of washing —
all we have learned to combat disease.
It is the churning steam and calm heat,
the spin of machines swiftly working,
carrying up heady herbal scents.
We give libations that glint in sunlight.
We give incense perfumed like steeped tea.
Bless us, Goddess, with goodness — drive out
illness as we purify spaces,
maintaining health and vitality.

To Asklepios

2020.

when you caught the secret
it was all-consuming
a spark igniting oil
sulfur alight in water
a desire to give the best
no longer watching
survivors' mourning laments
throwing themselves down
the dead a gaping hole within
children torn too soon away
women and men in their prime
cut down by disease and violence
you thought only of giving
flowing forth with unbound
providence from the far-darter
whose arrows cull and clip
whose harmonies bring healing
like a lyre you were
the great physician
and when your light shone
death could not cling to souls
so the swallower of all
sent lightning down to quiet you
the power igniting a fire
burning the mortality hot away
and your father welcomed you
brought you to Olympos
sweet nectar sudden upon you

drunk instantly at the feast
still the cries of lamentation
quicken your attentiveness
bestowing blessings from above
now knowledgeable of the weft
the weave of fate around all
of limit and unlimited
and the quiet place between

To Asklepios II

2020.

son of Apollon
your healing touch brings release
soothing aches and pains
brought by viral life

I said to you I'd compose
a prayer a poem adoring

when I wrote a hymn
years before hand-washing bloomed
bloody cracks across
chapped fingers each day

take this, giver of blessings
these words my notions made speech

a physician ascended
Asklepios opens gates
come to rest on stone
prayer perfumes the air

incense rises high
a pitch a note increasing

as we struggle here
in agons against disease
bring the scent of bay
medicinal arts

harmonizer of bodies
the drugs the vaccines are yours

the kisses of snakes
bring the shedding of old skin
renewing our selves
shaking decay away

come to rest, the balm within
a role a power repaired

The Birth of the Erinyes

2011 & 2020.

First, a cry —
a slash in the night —
a whisper — and hissing snakes
spat venom across the sky.
This is how the Eumenides were born:
from black Nyx sleeping
in the void between the stars.

First, a cry —
a stab in the dark —
a sigh — and then silence
dripping like rain onto the Earth.
This is how the Eumenides were born:
from a scythe of cold iron.

First, a cry —
a hole among the violets —
a scream — and a marriage.
This is how the Eumenides were born:
in a bed beyond the sun, where
roots meet liquid iron
and pomegranate trees sway.

First, a cry —
teeth gnashing in the dark —
a growl — and then blood money
denied to a family in grief.
This is how the Eumenides were born:

slighted Poine bore them in retribution.

First, a cry —
a lightless light blazing bright —
a song — one promise fulfilled,
another now long-forgotten.
This is how the Eumenides were born,
bringing harmony to long-lingering souls.

TO GE

2020.

Goddess who holds us close,
Ge humming with bees,
whose arms take in Ouranos,
pressing sky to primordial sea,
patchouli scent lingering
in the traces of nymphs' footfalls
while their branches dance.
We pray to you, Great Mother,
without whom life would not be,
lover of rain, giver of soil,
Goddess of chemistry and geology
keeping secrets in iron cores,
within the crustal waters of Europa,
at the plate boundaries on Earth,
tantalizing all with your power.
Help us move beyond consumption,
the rage of war, the pounding of iron.
Grant us the strength of heroes,
able to turn the tide of civilization,
hunting down each last spirit
running wild from Pandora's jar.
Assist us, O Goddess infinite
to whom each of us is but a mote,
and bring us into harmony again.

THE SUPPLIANT

I wrote this while in a study group (on a community site called BigTent that has since been discontinued) that was looking at Hellenic ethics and philosophy in 2011. I thank Mano and Lesley Madytinou for coordinating that learning experience. This poem was a reaction to Solon's tenets.

First bend your mind like a bow:
sense the aching, creaking wood,
and yield to the strength of seven
> *wiser,*
> *older, and*
> *more renowned,*

those adventurous truth-hunters.

Settle into that feeling
when you see someone in prayer,
when you hear good words on the street:
> *ruminate,*
> *meditate, and*
> *consider*

the roles you must play.

In years, repetition will make
your reason strong like the Gods.
You will follow them on paths
> *crooked,*
> *neglected, and*
> *well-worn,*

through deserts and rain forests.

They will leave you at the edge,
beyond which no mortal has seen.
A secret: the Gods are there, too,
> *hidden,*
> *visible, but*
> *waiting,*
and the oracle bones are in your hand.

For Apollon's Circle

2009 & 2019, *originally shared on the Kyklos Apollon listserv, an online prayer group that gave simultaneous Delphic dawn offerings every Sunday.*

I.

Come, God, from Delphi's navel.
Pass across raging oceans.
Find us here where we scatter
whole grain and speak sacred hymns.

This common purpose unites us,
like stars with their own systems
who yet dance together, the heavy
pull from the galactic center marking
out the rhythm in a great circle.

In your presence, life's hard road
metamorphoses into grass.
Cares diminish when we shout
ie paean; your oracular temple,
once location, now time, is
liberated by communal action.
God of the silver bow, hear
our praises and our thanks.

II.

Apollon, come from afar,
your Names are sacred.
From ancient precinct, Delphi,
to small modern shrines,
many worship you, keeping
the ritual hour.
Ever-vigilant, you once
kept black-robed Furies
from young Orestes.
Protect our minds; purify us.
Teach initiates
mindfulness, moderation,
and good discipline.
Before you all are equal,
all is made sacred.
For you we endeavor now,
Phoibos Apollon.
Thank you.

A Prayer for Rough Seas and Stalled Projects

2020.

I pray to the God who loosens,
steady night-thief breaking bindings,
Hermes — and to Dionysos whom no bond holds.
I pray to the Kharites, to the Horai,
O Great Athene who guides the warring soul,
champion of intellect over self-deceit.
I pray to the Mousai, to their mother,
to Far-Shooting Apollon of deadliest skill,
dancer upon wild mountain meadows, Chorister.
I pray to Hera who governs with steady scepter,
guiding Herakles through demanding labors.
I pray to the Goddess of endurance, Nike,
who bears valiant victory upon her shoulders,
to beckoning Amphitrite who knows the sea,
calm-hearted Goddess filled with serenity
no matter what tempest shudders the boundary
between sea and sky, drawing air into brine,
and to Poseidon, who holds the trident fast.

To all of you Gods — I pray for my work,
each project undertaken, each goal written out.
Rough seas tear my vessel across the waves —
my heart, sinking, fears for calm harbors lost.
Bind that heart steadfast to the mast.
Root it upward into cloud-swirling sky.
Keep me from the undertows of emotions,
anxieties, and desires that circle ever-dark,

old shames and passions that do not serve,
compulsions drawing me from prudent behavior.
Grant me habits that will be a calm compass.
May reason and planning lead me through
tumult to safe seas once more, nearing shore.
May my heart become a sail opening like wings,
guiding me in each action and deed, the mind
finding its rhythm as if dancing upon water.
To all of you Gods, I offer what I have.
May the gifts of my words and my actions
begin the process of finding firm ground.

FOR THE MOUSAI

2019.

I. Ourania.

Ourania, unutterable, you hold
the image of the sphere of Heaven.
Mnemosyne reflects the eternal sky,
and each measure of time is known,
counted, and described by you.
Constellation patterns are your first
mystery: on seeing them, wonder opens
the mind, drawing it up into your orbit.
You are most like your mother.
The night itself is another initiation:
souls, expanding up and out, lose
themselves in the blackness, in pinpricks
of light that spin and move in your sphere.
Playful one, you entice astronomers.
The beginning and the end constitute
your final mystery: expanding out,
the mind reaches limit, unlimited;
in the Λ and the $\dot{R}$ and the redshift,
you liberate all from our bonds,
our assumptions, our love of matter.
You hold the keys to mathematics,
to trigonometry, to the measures
cosmologists discern through probing —
a wide universe fit for a dance hall,
the light of stars so old we strain to see
how matter gravitates together,

how the vacuum renders all apart.
Vigilant one, you pull philosophers
beyond what is seen to look deeper:
Zeus holding his bright bolts high,
Hera bearing the crown and crest,
and the real dance beyond our images.

II. Erato

Erato — the most delicate
glances are yours in abundance.
O Goddess, you alone rule over
lingering gazes between lovers,
each drawn out, written carefully,
the tension driving each reader on,
this cascade of desire tumbling
like lovers playing in a bed of soft
down and thick-woven sheets.
To you we owe this captivation,
O companion of smiling Eros.
Your poetry draws the soul up,
beckoning, glancing backward.
Your verses oscillate like dancers.
O Erato, Mnemosyne bore you.
O Erato, Zeus taught you to dance.

III. Kleio

Kleio, you weave your stories tight,
be they sweet, bitter, or their mixture —
a Goddess who knows the tragedies

at each city's heart, you are the somber
companion of Athene and Zeus,
setting down memory with firm solidity.
You govern historians as they work late
hunched over texts and manuscripts,
deciphering old handwriting, making new
interpretations of what came before —
like conductors, each must deliberate
about the scores they will recount.
Your devotees perform everywhere:
in audiobook libraries, on city-bus tours,
or stacked and shelved in bookstores
for audiences' delight; to you belong
the archives built by all great nations,
swelling at the seams with ephemera
and data records of weather, famine, feast.

IV. Melpomene

Melpomene, out of tragedy
you make the greatest art —
laments that shake the spirit,
words that tear at our cores.
It takes skill to move a soul
so weighed down with matter.
We purify ourselves with tears,
the loss within us so very deep,
a hollow to be filled with more
decay or the all-living beauty.
In tragedy, a daughter dances,
flowers all around her, falls —
drawn down beyond the sun,

she becomes the bride of a king
to rise again as the crops renew.
In tragedy, a kingly child cut
down unfolds into lush fullness:
charmed with sacred mirrors,
killed without feeling the blow,
devoured by what divides us,
he is reborn again in stately ivy.
You purify all to receive this.
You gather the ivy, you wind it
tight around the staff, you sing —
and in the fullness of this sound
all releases into happy silence.

V. Terpsikhore

O Siren-mother, Terpsikhore,
you have pulled down beautiful forms,
locking each into gesture.
Dance is yours, from enraptured
planets held fast in stars'
gravitational
wells for all time
to artists
clutching
hands,
moving,
revolving
around a point.
Goddess, your sister
Ourania brings forth
mathematical secrets,

mysteries of geometry,
physics, each distillation of math;
you apply them, blossom impulse
into being — each triangle,
rectangle, circle, line —
applied sciences
your ballroom halls,
teaching all,
bringing
forth.
Beyond,
you delight
in each classroom
where knowing flowers
forth in abstract rhythm,
each intellectual exchange
a dance, words marking the space,
the rules and measures learned like steps,
until harmony sets in the soul,
discussions now shining head-wreaths,
harmonious and lively.
O Goddess, may we learn,
each hearing the beat,
feeling rhythm,
taking step,
filling
up.
O Muse,
Sotera,
bring us each
out of falsehood.
Grant us stable ground,
a sure education,

that ushers us swiftly
past unreason into light,
knowledge and poetry our guide,
from brambled wild to safe upward path.

VI. Polymnia

One still truth: There is no renown
flowering forth without the Gods.
We still recite the dedicated verses
written on soft-set clay tablets,
transcribed onto heavy papyrus,
cherished by the passing many,
millennia after each poet's burial.
O Polymnia, there is no renown
emanating forth without the Gods.
Each thing we compose and we give,
the sacrifices of intellect, of late nights,
preserves us through praising you.
The masses write light diversions;
those who remember and know you
travel the lonely path beyond them,
where we shed renown like snakeskin,
the mind unfolding into a window
refracting theogony and cosmogony,
symbol and signified, visions of each
God and of the churning all-Divine
brought down and braided into words.
You quicken us to receive this power.
Now, completion: There is no renown
dissipating forth without the Gods.
Even as we reach up to grasp you,

ego dissipates, burning up like seeds
that will never flower in the meadow,
love burning brilliant, bright, devouring.
Fame, at last, means nothing at all.
Better to fall silent than speak falsehood,
contort our prose, maim divine verse
— to sink back down in fragrant mud.
Best to give the world pantomime,
to hide in gesture without utterance,
O Goddess who rules silent and sacred.

VII. Euterpe

Euterpe, breath is central — flutes and pipes,
lips stretched firm, the diaphragm a bellows.
Unseen, you guided me for years while playing;
flautists all rejoice in this purest sound.
Lyric, too, relies on breath — our first one
that opens perspective, a sense of *I* —
discipline to learn the formal meters,
the blessings of a Goddess filling all
who make the air unfold like flowers bloom,
our each expression cultivated form.

VIII. Thalia

In the wilds beyond known pathways,
past the fields of dandelions shedding
forth their seeds as gentile as snowfall,
beyond the steady murmur of brooks,
the lowing of cattle, the bleats of sheep,

undiscovered springs gush symphonic.
Here, O Thalia, your meadow lies —
you dance among irises and sunflowers,
near pools where lily and lotus lie still.
All nature unfolds decadent, abundant,
the harmonious gladness of the world,
while beyond the mountains shimmer.
Flourishing Thalia, you bring power.
Poets who speak your name find voice,
setting names to this abundant beauty,
the cycle of seasons, the swelling of fruit.
Birdsong hymns honor you sweetly,
from theaters to homes to forest groves,
while the bees hum percussive for you.
In comedy, you marry delight, surprise,
and wonder; you mask and uncover all,
gleefully smiling, crying with laughter.
We will follow you to the far-off hills,
to the mountain, ivy-wreathed Goddess,
companion of Pan and dancing Eleutherios,
you who bear a shepherd's strong staff,
bringer of harmony, midwife of laughter.

IX. Kalliope

In epic, the soul strives up
to the still place beyond the cliffs
where mysteries are revealed
and the climber swallows secrets
hidden in shining egg and seed,
the structure of time itself,
signs set into mythic tapestries.

What eloquence, Kalliope,
you bring — commanding us,
driving attention to learn long passages,
verses as rhythmic as ecstatic drums,
truth found in the *Iliad*'s anger,
the journeying of the *Odyssey*,
and each work developed by skill.
What eloquence, Kalliope,
you bring — to the rhapsodes
who crown the words of poets,
embellishing and reworking tales,
acts of speech aging like fine wines.
Mother of Orpheus, giver of secrets,
eldest daughter of Apollon's chorus,
through you, we drive onward — up —
finding fast flight, driven by reason,
fine memories of fire and light,
skills that Mnemosyne has woven
within each of us that strengthen steady
as we yield to celestial melodies
falling like unencumbered curtains,
expanding everywhere, nowhere,
these epics of time that Orpheus
heard when he played and sang,
inspiring generations to write more.
Goddess, Muse, what eloquence
you bring — as we lift up,
give us stories well-tended as gardens,
fragrant as ever-blooming meadows,
and may we have the skill to bear
their complexity without falling
from the steep cliffs to break
upon the rocks in the river below.

TO APOLLON MOIRAGETES

2020.

Your drops of light slide immense
upon a plane yielding lightlessness,
chords descending taut-abrupt,
their labyrinthine infinity
hidden within harmony.

Pinprick notes bloom into asphodel,
the Sirens' sweet melodies,
rhythmic chant of the spinning Moirai,
as if you yet bind all being,
threads resonant, strung to the scaffold.

Here you delight Ananke,
O God who utters prophetic truth,
as you tune, O Apollon.
Your sevenfold harmony
wreaths all together again, lush, sweet.

God hidden in the pulsing,
rushing rhythm below-above sky
filled with twinned arrows dancing,
let our lots be like heliotropes
thick within the garden walls
following each trace and given cue,
each ecstasy of lightspring,
like laurel seeds we swiftly swallow.

To the Erinyes, Who Remember All

n.d.

Erinyes: we pray to you because you remember.
Erinyes: we pray for understanding of the ancient
practice — how to cool your rage with sweet honey,
milk, and blood to pacify the souls you represent.
Erinyes: we pray that you, lawyers in the court of souls,
accept the price we have paid for success,
those phantasms of gold dancing in our ancestors' eyes.
We may leave rare steak and milk at midnight,
but the memory of restless ghosts is razor-sharp.
The dead and dying remember all.
The dead and dying whisper in your heads.
The dead and dying bite at our heels.
Erinyes: give them the milk as a balm for their cut feet,
give them the rare steak to soothe their empty bellies.
May you and the dead accept our prayers.
May Persephone comb the snakes from your hair.
May you bathe in the soothing waters of Hades,
remembering always these sacrifices given,
and may we never forget the honors owed to you.

To Mnemosyne

2019.

Great Mnemosyne, powerful Titaness,
you hold the lake that bears your name.
Many claim to know you, yet grasp only
at ephemeral echoes within themselves.
Your waters are a vessel reflecting Nyx
back upon herself — you hold space so deep
within that it becomes abyssal, unending —
what was, what is, what has always been.
It unfolds shapeless, this image of time,
this totality of eternity in your gaze.
I taste your copper bitterness in prayer,
its traces of sweetness, and I know
the ebb and flow of this divine expanse.
Without dimension, it permeates all things.
Without opening our mouths, each knows
its scent, this nectar we always drink,
are *yet drinking*, as a white cypress
draws up from its roots in lamentation;
tethered down in matter, it seeks out
what is rained down to Earth from above.
I taste your copper bitterness in silence;
it coils around my tongue, the potential
ripping forth like lightning, fire, vastness —
the stories I have not yet thought through,
still trapped in the mazes of becoming.
Their shapes are there, lost in shadow.
To you belongs this meander through memory,
when past blurs to present and to future,

when the echo dissolves into the echoed —
the gift of words and language cannot
be gifted back to you, Unutterable One.
What *is* past, present, and future here
when you, Lady of Limitless Knowing,
gave birth to nine daughters from the one
who *knows* all things for all time — they
who dance to the lyre played by the God
whose prophecy hums in the soul like
the afterthought of a plucked string?
Hail, O Titaness, Child of Ge and Ouranos,
inventor of language, you of the bottomless
lake, O lady with your robe of bright stars.
Hail, Mnemosyne, and be well disposed.

HERA

2009.

You may know her from the sweep
of plains and the lowing animals,
cuckoos singing, nesting in baskets.
From her comes youth and discord.
From her all is born and fashioned.
From her you draw your first breath.
Look for her in the billowing white
bridal veil, the confetti of rose petals
falling on the floor, bruised underfoot.
For her you prepare wooden baskets.
For her you raise the goat's neck to cut.
For her you scatter the sacred barley.
Build her temples from windswept
beach sand, bear icons that call her
virgin, queen of heaven, and widow.
In her flit the birds and toys of steel.
In her the electrostatic charges meet.
Long before you worshipped her,
she gave birth: lightning passed through
her to strike primordial waters.
She is exhalation and inhalation.
She is the weight of the jungle air.
She is the humidity kissing your skin.
Know that she claims Rhea as mother,
Zeus the Thunderer as her co-ruler,
and her sons and daughters are many.

ERINYES

2017.

We make our beds in the land of knives
beyond the Styx among amaranth so sharp
its leaves cut through flesh, sinew, and bone
where our serpents can suck on dead marrow —
We have killed so many black lambs bleating
their last while stars scream the mourning cry,
shimmering beyond the cavern of night.

We come from the land of hate-cold waters
— dancing — reveling — entwining — processing —
live snakes enfolding our flesh, constricting,
their pebble-soft anaconda skin an aegis,
a journey we have made since the sickle sprayed us
through the night, when we fell, naked, crying,
onto the mountains then newborn in creation.

We three split the ground open and burrowed
like worms deep into its belly and rocky Ge
nurtured a hatred in us for the worst misdeeds.
We draw iron chariots for the broad-armed
Silent King and comfort the Lady of Sighs
when she spits pomegranate bones in the dust.
High are our honors: we know who you are,
all you have done, all your dust-ground
ancestors carried out, allowed, and unleashed.

Those who drip honey and leave raw wool
on our altars and initiates who wash sin away
with cake-ashes, we bless and offer liberation.
Those who know the Mysteries approach us
unblemished, hands and feet free of stains.
Flee from us if you dare: we run with the
owl-guarded queen to whom Zeus himself
gave highest honors among underworld Gods,
general of ten thousand million restless ghosts.

To Eris

2019.

Lady of blades and of apples,
of stratagems devised in retribution,
the clashes of bronze are yours,
strong words at marriage-feasts,
each cycle of anxious proofreading.
Daughter of Nyx, your insatiable
will drives all things into mixture,
as bright oil meets opaque water.
You are the one who draws on
the manacles of fate, cause-effect
as certain as any apple thrown;
these chains of years are countless.
You have thrown open the river
of division like a dam breaking.
You have set yourself upon the field,
rendering what was once an *us* apart.

O Relentless One, please relent.
O Taster of Blood, please let go.
O Lady of Sorrow, pivot this strife,
persuaded by Zeus and the Moirai.

Goddess, you delight in revolutions,
the unsettling of the quotidian
that jars us enough to look *up* —
poets have written so many words
of your harshness, not of your good.
You are the one who breaks open,

who overwhelms to make us see
divine truth that revolves, that is ever still,
as reliable as well-ordered mysteries
whose secrets grant salvation at midnight.
At the end comes recombination,
water cycling again to its source.

O Striking One, let the conflict
in our lives bring us to virtue's heights,
to good ends and hard-won unification,
accompanied by the healing gladness
the dancing Horai and Kharites bring.

To Horkos

2019.

Horkos, child of Eris,
you who enforces oaths,
playmate of Dike and Athene,
chaser of the Erinyes' serpents,
born on the fifth day
when the moon's slim sliver
begins to fill with silvery brightness,
let us uphold our oaths.
Bestow on us the strength
to drive ourselves onward
in pursuit of our promises,
away from shameful perjury.
Purify us of what was vowed
without our firm consent.
Trapped in dark ignorance,
these spectral oaths dissolve as
truth blazes sharply in our souls.
Grant us quick thought,
anticipating cause and effect,
so we may always be mindful,
even when unintended effects
shimmer like serpents in grass.

To Hermes

2009.

Maia gave birth to this
great rustler of mild bovine
animals, a thief
who operates under night's
deep indigo shield.
Cunningly, he flits among
those sleepers, bringing
wandering souls in line towards
the dreamer's wide vale:
Muse, let this brave God
receive worthy praise, renown
throughout the seven
continents, for his great work,
this walker between worlds.
Sing through me, paint myriad,
well-detailed accounts
of Hermes' exploits: recount
Argus's defeat,
retell the lyre's invention.
Such a noble God
deserves praise and sacrifice!
Hermes, please accept
humble words as your share.
Look kindly upon
your trim-ankled worshipper.

CDM

Previously published in *Astropoetica*, vol. 9(2), Summer 2011.

Keep climbing
out there
beyond oscillating planets and
hot stars.
Space is dark
like deep caves
where spiders burrow,
extended
without direction.

You are specks of dew
coasting down
radials
wrapped
in my body.
Blind,
you see nothing,
but you feel us moving
together.

No shame in this:
our real enemy
is the space where I cannot gather,
where I cannot hold you
together; a
vastness so cold,
deep,

profound
— hungering —
that it will gobble you up
and leave you childless.

To Hermes

2017.

Swift-footed, apt-tongued, wily deceiver,
Hermes born between underworld and sky,
karst-haunting, way-finding, keen diviner,
you speak in the murmur of water-drops.
Liminal realms are yours in abundance:
You know what lies illumined before you,
though many miss your light fingers darting,
thieving, intercepting oracles.
You catch glimpses beyond: Fate keeps her hair
shrouded in purple — the veil slips for you,
by stratagem or by design, with ease.
These cavernous places are yours, O Lord,
where water drips down through rock-pores to make
the sacred place where your mother once bathed.
Your first temple is here, shrouded in gold,
incense milling on the vaulted ceiling,
where the cradle once lay, from where you made
your first claims among the deathless on high.
I drink deep from the tortoise-shell goblets
and cleanse myself at your stalagmite gate.
In the shrine, your icon sits, bathed in rich
ambrosial droplets that send minerals
cascading down your chest and face, dazzling
like jewels from the ambient light grown hard.
Here, I pray that storms will be averted,
that you will guide me, even unseeing,
over the slippery stones, beyond lies.
Here, I pray that I always find correct

decisions, not deceived by the wrong paths,
as one finds jewels hidden in glass piles.
Here, I pray that you bless my armaments:
Those elastic spaces of meaning, words,
who always shift, slide, and metamorphose.
They find their images in ink and keys,
ama-iro and amber, moon-purple,
fast-drying, secret-keeping, drawn by pen,
or clacked out for consumption in spaces
without human touch, without human speech,
changed from alphabets to ones and zeroes.
Here, I offer this poem, written in both.
O clear-eyed wanderer, friend and guide who
offers warmth in the half-cold caves below,
hear me: Protect your devotee as our
world's bedrock rumbles and the dice roll on.

A Prayer for Endings

2020.

To which Gods do I pray
when the end draws near —
a blessed completion to projects
once thought long from over.
To all of the Gods, I offer thanks,
to those known and unknown,
to the patrons of intellectual skill,
the Gods who love two-ended-candle nights,
to the Mousai who rule the academy
alongside almighty Athene,
the Goddess who works through the night
without fatigue, whose wisdom remains sharp
no matter how many times it must cut,
to Apollon, the harmonizer and orderer of all,
to august Zeus and luck-bringing Hermes,
to the Horai and the Kharites,
Gods beneath the waves who guided this
even when all was uncertain, prone to failure.

To the unknown Gods I pray,
who dance at consciousness' edges like shadows,
iconographies mere wisps of smoke
playing at the human mind,
flashes of insights lightning-quick
as if Zeus still regorges the order of all.

I drink, you drink, the finest —
water — in relaxation.
I drink, you drink, the finest —

wine — in celebration.
I drink, you drink, the finest —
honey — in transcendence.

Thank you, O deathless ones.
The end of this project has come,
and my heart swells open with gratitude
like a flower releasing sweet pollen
to greet the springtime bees.

PART II

In the agora
she pulls up the kredemnon
thoughts bouncing like birds
hitting fabric boundaries
until, tired-winged, they
rest still as her tongue.

A Daily Prayer

2019.

I praise and hail you, Hermes,
you who walk in every marketplace,
in the agorae brimming with contact,
chance words, discussion, and violence.
Hail, O you who wander great cities' streets,
whose herms stand at their edges,
God who travels along the roadways in between,
lord of pastoral places and of flocks,
God found in the mountains.
Hail, herald of Zeus, you of flying sandals
who bears the staff, who makes elegant speech.
O Hermes, your companion is Persuasion.
Your tongue is sharp and fast-moving.
Rapidly, you think out thought.
Swiftly, your words break down distance,
you who know all languages
written, uttered, and thought.
Hail, my guide, my friend, my helper.
Please grant me success in the agora.
Please grant me protection due to travelers,
those of us who dare to make speech.

For Dionysos

2008.

Rush, you pressed from vines,
over the parched ground, moisten
our Gods' needy lips.
Once, before the torch-bearer
presented that first
gleaming krater, all danced through
life without passion
and the Gods knew not that high
offering. Then you came
from the mountainous east, hands
bearing green tendrils
while maenads danced in circles
crying "Evohé!"
You filled our cups then, and we
repay you with praise.

For Apollon

2008.

I know you. You ward
your devotees from afar.
You are the brilliant
God who fastens his soft hair.
Tell me, lord of light,
what offering pleases you most?
Hunger-sating zone
or wine splattered on icy
ground? You once enjoyed
hecatombs with votaries
whose long pilgrimage
meant a sacrifice no less
than the bulls slaughtered
on an altar bearing your name.
My skill with a knife
will not let me give what you
so rightly deserve —
Lord, consider a different
offering, a bloodless
hecatomb written to please
deathless minds and ears.
Like incense, may this give you
pleasure, radiant one.

To Zeus Who Releases the Rain

2011.

One evening, I biked along the back-country trail,
a liminal world between two counties where trains
had once gone, shaking nymphs from their slumber
as the cars whipped past the trees by the lake.
My legs stretched — pulled back — extended —
and I gripped the handlebars, fists like vices
while bike tires fumbled over the rough gravel.
Drops of unwelcome rain whispered against my skin:
a calm shower, nothing to run back home over, but
three miles from nowhere, out where the nymphs
still own the trees and land spirits murmur —
where I had yet to offer milk and nectarines —
thunder rumbled and dark clouds blanketed the west.
Zeus raised his cup in a libation for the thirsty land.
His breath raised a wind that shook the branches.
My feet touched the cold ground where muddy
puddles collected on the dirt-and-stone trail.
As rain speckled my clothes, I whispered a prayer
to the God who holds the thunderbolt and the sky,
he who freed the Kyklopes from their dungeon.
An opaque wall of gnashing rain marched
down the trail — thunder cried — lightning streaked — ;
I spread my arms to embrace the Thunderer.
Zeus pelted my arms and my face with his rage.
Somehow, I escaped, but not before awe soaked me
to the bone and I remembered, as my ancestors
knew in their hide huts and element-naked shelters,
the power of the Gods who animate all things.

EXACTERS OF JUSTICE

n.d.

Our ebony Erinyes have remained unyielding since
spilled blood sprayed them across the heavens.
As babies, they played with hooded snakes.
As children, they wielded spears and swords.
As women, they now keep the peace of the dead.
Exacters of justice, like a fire they sweep through the land,
black as scorched ground, our growling night-cats.

Five Poems for Athene

2017.

I. To Athene

Strong-voiced Athene, champion of Heaven
who stands proud at the lightning-bearer's side,
would that I could hymn you as deftly as those
psalm-paraphrasing women we read, tomes
marking out a space where women could write
without fear of their male kin's reprisal.
Religion has always been an enclave
veiling women so we can move freely.
They wrote those devotional poems and prayed.
Long before them, women took up weaving.
Women wove and carried your sacred gifts,
garments to adorn your gleaming statue.
Well-hymned Athene, in these woven words,
I come up to the image of your shrine.
Creatrix of law, codes, regulations,
and the juries that rule humans and Gods,
cities weep when you show them your judgment.
Virginal and austere, you lift up ones
whom you love and cast out the offensive.
Bright-eyed Athene, Olympian, come —
pivot away the aegis on your chest!
Leave those weapons in your relations' care.
Come, whether your attention is in courts
or governmental halls of great countries.
Come, O lover of learning and its halls,
you who hold up philosophers and grant

quick thought and cunning alongside Hermes.
Come, O Athene, to this place, accept
these words lain out at a devotee's shrine.

II. Thoughts on Deacy's Athena

It is night, Athene,
quiet at this shrine where your
icon stands covered in the piece I made,
blue as the harbors you protect,
gray-trimmed like your calm eyes.

Athene, vexations
swirl me about, analysis
I never knew before — it accused you,
said you had betrayed all women,
diced you into pieces.

This has occupied me,
glowing candle-steady, and now
I want to hymn you and weave other tales.
You are more than a plot device
steering along strong men.

Goddess, when I found you,
I loved you instantly and saw
you knew what being *the girl among boys*
meant: making a hard shell over
unwillingly touched skin.

That takes strength, Athene.
It requires fortitude to take

battering ram words from other women.
I know how hard striking balance
in those moments can be.

It still mystifies me:
Why did those mortal women call
themselves better than you? You built cities.
To them, it made you less skillful
at the loom. Shame on them.

You protected people
like Nikandra, a weaver who
needed to feed her family with wages
she earned by spinning long hours.
That aid helped buy her bread.

That nuance explains why
criticism against you hits
sore nerves in my heart, but I keep reading
because something in there
must be fit for your shrine.

It is night, Athene,
and I offer up thoughts for you
out of a promise I made due to careless
words spoken — because you deserve
respect. It's what you're owed.

III. Three

Three, which we
name sacred.

Athene
counts out three.
Three, the day
set down by
calendars
to be yours.

This playful
interlude
separates
troubled thoughts
from what comes:
Praise, stories,
gratitude,
and still more.

IV. To the Foresightful, Inventive One

Mekhanitis, from wherever you roam,
be it mountainous Olympos held dear by all,
senatorial hallways, your Athenian overlook,
or a secret place where you, done with battle,
remove that glorious armor and set down
sword and spear to wash the blood away —
come, O you who are good at strategy,
advice-giver, protector, sharp-sighted maiden,
you who govern all things according to plan.
O Aider of Girls, you instruct all in practical
measures for increasing industriousness.
You, Mekhanitis, worked with Orion's daughters,
and the tapestries they wove revolve in Heaven.
You, Mekhanitis, work with all inventors,

teaching us what must be done in our crafts,
setting the power of the mind to demarcate
our creations and imbue them with skill.
To you we make libations of your sacred oil;
from you, we have the holy scent of olives
seeping into our thirsty skin, parched throats,
and tired muscles, until we become supple,
quick-bodied and quick-thinking, foresightful,
all thanks to the blessings of that first tree.
Illustrious Parthenos, you elevate souls,
soothing the body so that we may write thoughts
according to reason with smoothness in our hands.
Please, O Goddess, accept this prayer of praise.
May your favor be as sweet as the delicious,
grassy oil you have given for our benefit.

V. To Athene Mekhanitis

The incense burns down, Athene,
on this shrine where your offerings
pile, ash over ash, in the bowl.
Mekhanitis rolls from my tongue.
This epithet makes me think of you
alone, your luminous face glowing,
lit only by orange-red emergency
lighting on the walls of your lab.
It evokes smoke-curling images
where you draft out designs on
large papers spread across tables.
I see you building, fingers tipped
with grease, aegis facing backwards
so people are afraid to interrupt.

Women's work has changed so much.
Wherever we work with deft hands
belongs under your wide shield.
Women streamed into factories and
offices where we typed up notes
or fed garments through machines
— always with accurate posture —
and on to other places where we
make our studios, writing desks,
law firms, and highway truck homes.
We still manage households at night,
defend ourselves from those who want
actions brushed aside and not seen,
and deal with those who would slight
our achievements as worth less.
I see you, Mekhanitis, diligently
working until the night grows drowsy.
You watch over women who come home,
O gray-eyed one, and direct wrath
towards those who would harm us.
Women are steel-hearted and invent
ways to economize and pare down,
essentializing things that once took
all of our ancestors' long days.
These are devotions to you, Athene,
at the shrines we call city streets,
the temples we transform from offices,
complete with desks where we offer
time and roadways where we chariot race.
Mekhanitis, austere and finely-clad,
professional patron and guide,
you have brought me so far in my love.
What I know about wisdom, you taught me.

You have set lightning in my head,
so fast is this storm of thoughts.
I thank you for the breaths curving
my ribcage and diaphragm, the incense
I can purchase due to your favor,
and the many opportunities you grant.
The incense has burned down,
and still my hands face outward
towards the icon at your shrine.

NINEDAY

2019.

A Saturday — the first forgiving morning
following months of sharp winter gales —
I bound my hair back, a single headband
holding in the wildness women bring forth.

The blue jar bore a mark of cold water
condensation, a dividing line, filled;
the incense perfumed the air even
before lighting like a delicate bonbon.

I prepared the reading for your day,
Goddess of the cymbals and drums,
mother of the deathless, purifier of all
who freed her hair when Kronos fell.

They came when I had the lightning
lighter out; the doorbell sounded.
USPS, perhaps — a second ring, though.
More insistent. I stopped the lighter.

Two at the door. One young, waffling,
uncertain of himself, the other practiced,
both a disorganized mess of three ring
binders, pamphlets drawing down Khaos.

Is this what I stopped the worship for?
Rhea, O Queen, my steady protector,
I told them I already had salvation and

we all stood there waffling, but they left

because who could argue with that?
In annoyance, I walked back upstairs,
miasma of arborescence coiling, my heart
asking if I'd said the right thing — yes.

It was to be a morning like all others,
the rhythm of the lunar month manifest,
sacred to the Goddesses who dance freely,
cooling their thirst in Parnassus' springs,

to far-shining, all-remembering Helios,
last to you who transition orders of Gods.
The verses called you Purifier; I asked you
to drive back the pollution of my thoughts.

From the window, they were stopped doors
down milling in the street, discussing
or in supplication — I hope not for me.
Do I possess salvation or did I lie to them?

I am pure through you, Lady of Lions.
Your Orphic hymn calmed me. It bore witness.
It saved me from the bitterness circling,
triangulating every missionary encounter.

The incense burned slow, soft-scattering,
dissipating into the air while springtime
sun filled the apartment, soft and joyous,
marking prayerways I have always known.

THE NAMES OF GODS

2018.

A name winds like a riverbed,
its syllables overflowing,
sediment layers of offering
tablets we've stored in temples,
old language beneath the new.

We have spoken Greek for so long.
When you came to our homeland,
you fastened a peplos around her.
Athena brushes our tongues
against the back of our teeth.

We make statues and paint vases
showing the virgin city-maker,
yet beneath the red figures
is clay from our own rivers,
when we called her *Maliya*.

You braided her hair and brought
her down from the mountain,
severed her from rivers and horses.
Names of Gods are like riverbeds,
easily traversed by diplomats,
rudely forced when soldiers follow.

No one speaks Lycian anymore.
Perhaps in time, that name will sink
down in sediment like Hittite.

We remember, even as *Athena* curves
our tongues, even as the river flows
placid, ever consuming new names.

Ge Adorns the Suns with Rings

2019.

Powerful Ge, Earths uncountable
dance untethered, limitless —
deep seas of tidally-warmed moons
worlds who greet vivid dawns
all adorning host suns
meadows of green and gray
tracing out paths in habitable rings.
Goddess, your spinning brings
magnetic fields, those hundred-handers
from within your womblike cores.
Alongside young Zeus, they castrate
solar winds, casting particle jets
like blood into Ouranos' thick domain
where they shine bright
like sickles and sea-foam.
Goddess, be kind to us —
may flares never flow fiery upon
our Earth, may chance and Fate
keep asteroids at bay
may limitless life blossom forth
symmetric in its churning
our dance of birth, consumption, death
bodies sheaths for weary souls
to ground ourselves
while we gather strength
to turn back, to draw up.

For Mnemosyne

2020.

within the heavens
light unfolding bottomless
reaching to touch Earth
who turns and circles

you extend to Kore's grove
a drop a vastness starlit

what changes remains
current-driven, deep, shallow
this stillest water
this wide labyrinth

Mousegetes once drank deep
a rhythm a crown his claim

no leader until
this liquid gave sovereignty
all chords his temples
not yet remembered

the Mousai he leads to sea
a bow a lyre seeding

nine and three and nine
daughters nourished upon thought
its traces echoes
witnesses of time

now they gather in the grove
a dance a movement of bees

For Cosmic Artemis

2019.

Artemis dances, encircling, turning.
She counts out the shape of eternity.
Her forms and movements, aionic measures,
make the beginning and limit of all.
Everything she does is with boundless grace,
descending with vibrations like footfalls.

Beyond those heights, marking sacred measures,
her brother's firm count reflects her turning.
She, the Hunter of Hours, captures all
as she draws back her bow with quiet grace,
this Devourer below eternity,
where among the nymphs echo her footfalls.

Her song is the tension, the binding; all
know it, the flower of eternity.
In the forest, in the meadow, her grace
contains each thing, the sinusoid turning,
ascent and descent arrow-bound measures,
the generations she slays as footfalls

murmur in the mountains; she kills with grace
before bringing back into birth us all.
We are born again in Ge, whose turning
creates abundance, power — these measures
held within the archer's eternity.
Bright Goddess, still, traveling, your footfalls

sound from high summits to the deep-turning
ocean ravines, divine one, bearing grace.
You hold the boundary of eternity,
Aionic, Khronian, untied, Great All;
with each prayer, the soul transcends its measures,
and your inner sanctum swells with footfalls.

Your being opens into depth, no measures,
so sublime it tears breath away and all
fall silent as your fire flowers; you grace
us with shimmering knowing through turning
to look up at star-filled eternity,
at space beyond space, a hall without walls.

For Apollon Without Measure

2019.

Apollon, in moments before we breathe,
you are measureless — you are beyond time —
then the harmony begins like a swan
descending smooth upon cold-still water.
It opens the way for your harmonies,
sinusoids and vibrations bringing light,
drawing nearby end to far beginning,
at once primordial, knotted, unseen,
giving birth to order and steadiness
where brightness can draw together at last.

Upon your brow fragrant laurel limbs wreathe
whose scent awakens the desire to climb.
Equations divined like organs have drawn
so many; atoms offered for slaughter
in caverns below universities
find symbols so melodious, bright,
concordant as a new planet spinning.
Deftly, each string so taut, each one your mean,
now vibrates in feathery heaviness,
for a dance in this universe so vast.

Mirror

2020.

Speak,
O Mousai,
of Mnemosyne,
your mother who brings within
herself the form of eternity
as if she had swallowed all
before her wholly.
Declare her
child
of Aither
anoint her daughter
slipped to Ouranos by Ge.
Long before Zeus sowed you within her,
she brought Nyx into herself,
the mother of all,
she who holds
keys
that open
a ballroom holding
burning stars, galaxies turning fast.
As a mirror entrances,
when Nyx beheld her,
heart dancing,
she
stopped driving
her swift chariot.
Nyx knelt beside the still lake,
tracing over its waters with thumbs.

This gentle touch sent ripples
shaking through the calm
depths that knew
no
gaze upon
the vastness, no touch.
Mnemosyne reached up to pull.
She grasped Nyx by one slender wrist and
brought the Goddess down to her.
The pattern of stars
opened up
quick
projecting
down the lightless night,
flying like a hum of bees,
seeding Mnemosyne with tokens
faint as shadows drawing breath,
destined to unfold
poetic.
Sky
to waters,
fingertips stretching,
pressed together with lithe limbs,
divided, undivided, union,
a prophecy of moments
afterimages
spilling forth
bliss,
no children
conceived but hollow
images, these hands and channels signs
Zeus would uncover complete
when he bestowed you

upon her
yet
beloved
of that gentle queen,
giving form to the patterns.
How you dance, O Mousai, how you sing,
filled with divine harmony,
seeded from sameness
now brought to
light.

Light-Scattered Fire Upon Us

2019.

oscillating as if struck
a singularity of harmony
beginning unfathomed anew

we opened up like a maw ready
all that came before swallowed
into the place that yet sings

give birth, sweetness, give
there is no seed in Ge's house
but what her vessels pour out

sudden bright electric moving
the limit a being without edge
light-scattered fire upon us

still it quenches itself dark
there is seed in the shadows
a flower grows tall enmeadowed

in this steady sequence of rulers
past only visible through Zeus
empowered, sceptered, enthroned

feel the static on your hands
clear as Hubble photographs
gritty as the Planck images

hydrogen and helium make light
supernovae disgorge massive metals swift
what violence gives are tools for war

hear the knife as it falls on Zagreus
the shadow of a God's stable reign
the popping, space itself pulling apart

will a new coronation come up
tomorrow unfathomable again
after constant change is cut down

To Apollon of the Steep Cliffs

2020.

Apollon who holds the steep cliffs,
unfathomable, whose agalma
is the edge of the event horizon
at which light dissipates out,
known and unknowable, an edge
yet permeable, I pray to you, O beacon,
O rainer of arrows whose bow sings,
O God whose nectar is pulsar-scream gusts
colliding within and without us.
I pray to you, O Apollon of the field,
who sings out the tapestry woven
by Persephone in her hidden cave,
serpentine God ever out of sight,
the omphalos a weight binding all
down against the navel of Ge.
How to hymn you, O God, when place
becomes estranged from itself,
unplaced, without creating
sacred topographies of sound and echo,
above all deep silence, lightlessness
yet humming with quantum noise —
as if we have followed Daphne
deep into the thickets of redshift
where the past lies frozen as future,
postcognition an oracle of depth,
the laurel we reach out to touch
dissipating on the river of inky darkness,
the steep cliff of photons beyond it
yet desiring the future, looking back.

If we trace you to the high root,
time collapses into your eternity,
all chords sung in union together,
and beyond that is all hum and note,
your retinue a wave of everything
moving in place, vibrating sweet,
yet unfathomable as bowshock,
this drum of words within my mouth,
this ground beneath my feet falsely still.
I have found the eversmooth cliffs.
I have heard the black hole's hollow
incantations beyond its sharp boundary.
May my words bear flight to you,
touching you with praise, O God.

Plasma Veils

2019.

Helios' daughters shield all life;
the eldest took Earth as a bride.
Together, they embrace and guide,
enshrouding all in bright fire
to keep life safe from every strife
— cosmic rays like arrows pouring,
while within the winds are raging —
Goddesses whose grace all admire.

WHAT IMAGES WE MAKE

2018.

The strongest agalma is the amalgam of the mind
arising from prayers, thoughts, and offerings.
A God is the lock; the mind-in-pattern its key.
These forms, forged thoughtways, shift mercurial —
now a guest house for the bow-bearing Twins,
then for the Guide who loosens his sandals.
A God flows into any space like limself[1] easily,
like water filling a jar, electric current in wire.

Yet if the mind makes these images, take care —
do not bind up what cannot be released again.
A writer once said that in the agora of ideas, so I say:
Chase after pollution that deserves no name,
that which hungers after epithets, the devourer,
and it will colonize one's brainstem like rot.
Here, the images the mind creates will distort.
Here, as it consumes, you will see it everywhere.

Take care of the images and weed the garden.
Allow into the mind who and what Solon once said
make for happy company, name the Purifier your guide.
Apollon once said to *know thyself*; this true root
will bring nothing but gladness even though digging
causes pain and hardship as we see our own selves.
Fill yourself with good images and ideas — strengthen
the mind's key, and you will not break it in the lock.

---

[1] A singular pronoun based on the one suggested by Edgar Alfred Stevens in *The Current* in 1884.

For Mnemosyne the Wayfinder

2020.

Mnemosyne in the heavens
accompanying the Mousai
who dance splendid-liquid
in the house of their father,
you stir the recollection of love,
you move appetites to ends.
I see you in the twist of DNA,
the stories rocks bear in strata.
Light from far-off stars heralds you,
and you are yet below in lightlessness,
Goddess, accompanying Kore
before you return to your home
and the lake of vivid quietude.
In the beginning, your nine daughters
dwelled within your waters
until they grew strong, feet quivering,
hands moving fast, voices stirring,
as if your stillness had dawned moving form.
At Mousegetes' birth, you brought him
to drink from your bottomlessness,
crowning his heart with mousikē,
ascendancy over arts to perfection.
He led your daughters to Delphi,
across the sea where souls fight the waves,
beyond the tall mountain forests,
to the steep peaks embracing sky.
Hear me, Goddess, accept this prayer:
Grant memory, poetic skill,

the steadfastness to wayfind through
mazes of passages within these books,
tracing out what was once written
on woven papyrus and smooth vellum,
writers' hands grasping ink-dyed sticks,
dictated in halls unknown to this life,
copied to save them, translated.
Goddess, may you, Apollon,
and the Mousai bless this effort,
bringing only good things
as if my body were fertile soil
and my mind were a sunflower
hymning you by turning,
by breathing in, exhaling, becoming.

To Rule: A Meditation on the Choice of Paris

2019.

the bee chose sovereignty
sweetest nectar of all
in the yet-fragrant orchard
pink and white blossoms giving forth
long before the fruit swelled gold
all that could be given
to rule and know the love of rule
and if this queendom falls
devastation, devastation, collapse

Reflections as the World Falls Apart

2020.

all below lustrous
an Apamean sun hot
dew on fine statues
sublimating quick

Muses' faces deep wellsprings
a hum a song ruptured sharp

Time limself[2] dances
those ruins half-remembered
crumbling cornerstones
sand whirls in harsh winds

all that remains is eclipsed
a promise a curse rending

we buried our hearts
like Dionysos' remains
as the temples burned
as we burned with them

they march now on Earth herself
still the fire roars unceasing

---

[2] A singular pronoun based on the one suggested by Edgar Alfred Stevens in *The Current* in 1884.

my blood rushes up
place unplaced within without
lacuna-filled strife
a world inverted

now how to turn back, to heal
hum envesseled bond restored

Δ

2020

Apollon, you bear
truth within your gleaming hands
cascading like streams
yet still as held breath
like the fruit hidden
within its husk to open
such fragrant nectar
heady with laurel

its taste unfathomable
it is the murmur of bees' songs
the dance they make upon discovery
the flight of nymphs

the rustle of old bay leaves
dry within the drawer
popping with fire as the smoke rises to you

your mother grasping a palm tight
as she bears you to the world upon Delos
while your sister cries the birth-cry
her hair already fragrant with flowers
her feet already hungering for flight

it is the weight of the not-yet-lyre
each holy utterance that fills the mouth
dancing with unborn potentiality

yet within this — simple
finer than spider-silk caught in sunlight
an edge the human hand cannot grasp

we cannot measure beyond
the Planck length where all breaks down
and all that's left is trust
our ability to breathe deep
to swallow truth into our lungs
as if feeding the roots of our minds
the vivid melody within
drawn out by you

it is so simple to pray for truth
to catch that delicateness
open palms reaching out
your image always-smiling
echoes of your mother, sister, father
humming in the heart as we speak

deception a sickness
we shake the fever out
you bring the balm, the healing verses
we open up in tactile serenity

may we follow you up the pathway
drawn together into ourselves
our perceptiveness ordered
from shaking bone to anxious mind
replaced with equilateral steadiness
a clear center at our hearts

To the Horai

2019.

Daughters of Themis, you who flow,
Goddesses who dance on the mountainsides
on your rocky path to the shadowy cave
where your sisters count out fate's measure,
offspring of Zeus, the sovereign who
ordered this paradigm into being,
you who follow Helios, hear these words:

Goddesses, you are the patrons of goodness.
You set human souls into flourishing,
fertilized by divine roots that run so deep.
Hear my prayer, easy-living ones, for people —
we are buffeted on all sides by these winter
storms, as if Eris has plunged her knife down,
two millennia of inertia, curses, and strife.

Eunomia, you who have made the sense
within our hearts of right and wrong,
the balance of conformity and individuality
that sets the bounds of the fertile fields
of our souls so all may grow in our turns,
please sow community within us,
reverting all to proper balance under you.

Dike, firm-hearted Goddess whose justice
penetrates all things, companion of Athene,
yours is not a will that bends under pressure.
As a child, you played with the Erinyes;

you developed respect for their venom.
Please bring us into conformity with
fair judgments and laws, ever watchful.

Eirene, sower of peace, you who carry
the fruits of hard-won labor forward,
who give out all in due accord with effort,
you pacify Ares with your words' kindness.
To you belongs the season of risks, when
strategy is most dear; please grant us favor:
let soothing words in the agora pacify all.

Ephemerality — Justice — Love

2019.

I. Ephemerality

trajectory unstable
wandering stars   fleeting souls
laws changing planets spin

pages geologic seams
rules mutable rules static
we process we precess

opinions gathered data
models mirror   minds create
symmetrical alive

II. Justice

to Dike most just
we pray for honest nations
states undeceiving

grant inspiration
wisdom to our officials
freedom from falsehood

with the Erinyes
your companions, hunt hubris

reward blood with blood

with sweet Eirene
bring peace to online spaces
sow virtue in stone

justice eternal
in union with Hephaistos
swift encircuited

may newfound laws bind
the polity electric
nothing escapes you

III. Love

Eros who binds root to sky,
soothe the heart loud-pattering.
In prayers we give freely,
incense circling high.
Light the lampway leading up,
down, and out with the sizzling
static of the one who holds us,
these quiet acts of speech
a unity of syllables reverting.
What vile impulses can you
banish if not cruelty,
the love of hurting one another,
desire for pain and suffering,
pleasure in misfortune and death?
Eros, holy and pure, lovesick,
in the company of Eirene,

build in us a love wondrous
pouring fire from above-within,
until the vileness burns
to ash glistening in sunlight,
the samskaras slumbering deep.

ONLINE AGORAE

2019.

Swift-speaker, the Internet is sacred ground
made from the intangible
trapped in liminal underground cables,
connecting data centers,
traversing land, air, and sea.

Instead of incense, the masses offer
Bitcoin and copper wire,
Pinterest image boards loud-colored
and vibrant with a thousand
iterations of your face.

In this place, may we find solace from bloody
matches in these faceless agorae,
where some scream to be heard and
others shout us into silence —
a visit from Ares is a woman's undoing.

We find the *kairos* of your oracles in feeds
as they stream by, words scrolling,
eyes taking in a thousand
futures, making connections,
selecting and unsubscribing.

Your choruses in this ephemeral world are
Tumblr reblogs meandering their stories.
Gods delight in retelling,
in the mingling of ideas,

in this speedy, mind-drowning place.

I veil myself so I may move unhindered,
never speaking until thinking,
always treeing out possible actions,
reactions, in the analog
way station in between.

Protect me, you who know your
way through the noisy mire.
Translator, help me make myself heard
accurately, be a friendly face
in these digital spaces.

Concord, Faith, Harmony

2019.

this prayer a dividing line
limit unfurling unbound
the pinprick of the mean alight

in pursuit of stately concord
to Athene whose grace shines
your stern smile dispensing

soft power compelling all
fasten us to the perimeter
quicken etiquette, virtue

I pray for people, listen —
a sharp wind carries us down
a thread can bind if woven

Goddess with bladed intellect
interwork mind to breath to bone
still the all-hungering storm about us

virtue's triple Sun shines sharp
this beacon beyond time itself
truth and love inviolable mortar

O Horai, born from Themis
O Horai, who limit all things
O Horai, who measure the hours

echoes of divisions visible
a trace of instants past and future
threads spun by your hidden sisters

faith is the vital rod running
deepest root to flowering sky
flooding mire with bright bolt-light

through it hardening into virtue
strengthening into bedrock stone
still the wind howls so strong

let it come unmoving at last, O Horai
begin the healing rains, O Horai
flow forth with katharmos, O Horai

at the meeting-place Harmonia
reveals the bitter tension of peace
sanctified with a necklace of strife

Hephaistos, radiant metalworker
fashioner of the sheath of bodies
adorned with the raiment of the soul

restore the fruit to the vine unsinged
cosmic balance teetering nevermore
I pour out separation into steady union

if all ends in strife, what ascent
God, send forth the blazing chariot
return your daughter to shining Polias

may concord reign in our world
may faith be the stable place within
may harmony reign beyond division

Part III

Taken, I am poised,
the strong arrow in your bow.
Turn me where you turn.
Aim me where you have most need,
and when your fingers
let me fly, I rest knowing
a stable path holds.

Acts of Speech

2019.

Incense lit, electricity dancing
pole to pole — my thumb presses out prayer,
an act of speech as natural as breath,
passing up, circling out, diffusing far.

Forbidden for so long is smoke as thin
as exhalations, the quiet utterances,
dancing circling perfuming the agalma
who shines in morning light as stick-ash curls

down, taut as Apollon's bent bow, to rest.
My mind sends out branches thick as the years
of spent sticks in this bowl. I rise with you.
Carry my words, O scent that blossoms forth.

You may have started a spring-born bloom,
a nymph's tears as she watched great ruins burn,
or ground down from fragrant bark — ending *here*,
blended tight, extruded, brought here to me.

This act of speech I witness in silence.
My fingers find your pulse on calm mornings,
ecstatic nights, those days when hardship rends,
moments when joy soothes me back together.

Like Cassandra

2019.

At the sunrise of this strange life
Apollon slid a split tongue deep,
kissing my eardrums with fever.
Fluid swelled, blessed by Hekatos.

The hollow early hours of morning
are what I remember, sitting in bed —
infection pounded driving beats
that persisted despite my tears.

Years of this knitted scar tissue tight.
And yet I have seen the midnight sun,
yet I have climbed the ladder lain
unwatched, all from that platonic kiss.

The Cosmos — Void — Night — Radiance

2019.

I. The Cosmos

O God, I have no laurel for a crown.
The dust of dried leaves lies at my feet
in this library whose volumes are countless.
Here are the traces of all that I know,
yet I open the pages and tear them out.

Curled into flowers, strung together,
they succumb to perfection as the words wind.
Such delicate leaves — patterned with passages
like rivulets cascading across barren ground
as fire split the rocks of primordial

Earth apart, its texture like the scent
of stone beneath my hands as my fingers
trace across it — I slide them into place.
You who draws all things together, come
through my lips like bees to their hive,

fill my mind that opens like a bowl.
Let my hands bear the power of speech,
let my head be worthy to make this crown.
You are the one who set particles into
tuned harmony at the beginning of creation,

the quarks and electrons, neutrinos shot
from afar dancing rhythmic oscillations.
The brightness of galactic nuclei are yours,
the particle jets that curve like bows,
new stars' bow shock, the screams of pulsars,

the concord of solar systems, the bright
music of supernovae, of inspiralling bodies.
The end and the reunion are yours, too —
the quiet dance of particles as they die,
as matter dissipates in soundless light.

II. Void

In this broken ground we call home,
this place where shadows softly creep,
who watches the night as it shifts deeper,
this change of the seasons, the blessings
of twisted corn-stalks in the fields?
When I was a girl the fireflies strobed.
The sky above our heads was a temple.
The first image I had was a Goddess,
skin star-studded, night-black like Nut,
like Nyx, not-Nut, not-Nyx, someone
whose name remained in shadows of pages
not yet read, lost in unfathomable sea.
The curve of her face, the arms raised,
said *bottomless* and I tasted copper
and steel like water left long sitting.
I felt the vacuum in her, the expanse
that took my breath away on clear nights
when star led to nebula led to depth

unfathomable to my mind, body forgotten,
the swell of the sun into Earth-devouring
giant yawning as I contemplated that all we
know would give way to it, all was hers.
What name to give to a Goddess who takes,
who holds aloft our creation, dissolution,
who preserves our echoes like etchings?
I felt the night as it deepened then,
the bottomless water that reflected stars,
fields of asphodel that had never seen sky.
Memory, then, who holds the future and
past, whose lake swells like an inkwell
overflowing, giving birth to creative art.
Mnemosyne, then, whose black lake reflects
the beauty of Nyx, so gentle to touch,
whose water is unfathomable to swallow.

III. Night

I found Nyx in a poster.
Who knows what I thought,
a child, as I saw her floating,
all good things edging
along her body as she drove
her nightfall over the Earth.
I did not understand the
delight that captivated me,
the way I moved the paper
carefully until carelessness
and moves wore it down,
often — or always — enshrined.

IV. Radiance

We made river-clay sculpture, scent heavy
with our floodplains, small stones
the price paid for within-budget art.
In school, my hands never made icons,
but vessels, as even then I knew
I would need all I could for holding.

Later, I hollowed out my words,
beat them firm until they held shape.
In this fertile valley, I learned
the counts of syllables from fireflies,
how to form each line for the kiln,
the ways that the memory of Gods hum

in the back of one's mind like beloved
places now forgotten — we are all
seeded from cataclysm, united here
to solar afterbirth as it encircles our
stars, scar-patterns visible from afar —
the traces of them in our souls unseen.

Your light caught me finding verses.
I breathed into these words, opened their
meaning like a mouth to hold you dear,
and they bent for you, taut as a bow,
until your shape danced like sunlight
and I recognized you in that gladness.

The jars taught me how to hollow out,
how to shape, how supple mud and argil

yield to practice, to familiar likenesses.
The body is like river clay, how it yields.
In the shapes of syllables, in the count,
in the cymbal-clash and the silence,
I pour out, give way, light rushing — a flood.

LIKE A KNIFE'S EDGE

2019.

As a child, I flew kites on the hillsides,
grass green and endless until it met the knife-edge
of sky at the horizon line, that endless blue.
In my mind's eye, you dance on those slopes,
making circles with one another, O Goddesses.
Kleio, Euterpe, Thaleia, Melpomene,
Terpsikhore, Erato, Polymnia, Ourania,
Kalliope — with you nine I begin,
the multicolored veils shrouding your faces,
never lifted back, concealing laughter and silence,
the song that begins with the first quiver
of matter shaking through the Big Bang,
the long hold stilling here, then there, as rests
take hold of the composition,
these sacred springs that hold your
inspiration and purification
drawn forth like oceans of light breaking
waves onto the rocky shores of the mind,
pregnant with foam and form.
Your mother is Mnemosyne, O Goddesses,
that powerful Titan who maintains all in eternal reflection.
Your father held the world within himself,
gave birth to all that came before and after.
To you he gave the plan through the memory of
        Mnemosyne
whose lake tastes of bitterness
as deep as infinity unbounded,
its shores as perimetered as limit itself,

a divine sign within the arts that bring truth.
O Goddesses, you dance the rounds
of purification granted by Apollon,
you who trace out the whirl of his pattern,
you who bring forth memory into action.
I look up into this sky, this endless blue,
a depth wholly unlike you, wholly like yours,
and the dance in my soul is harmony.

Solstice Dawn

2019.

the darkest night
eyes sleep-tinged, hair perfumed
by the soft bonfire we lit outside

when they say *stay*
up until the dawn creeps in
know your mind will be cotton-white

like the cloudy sky
and we will only see glimmers of sun
it is still winter as light rises

ritual drum memories
strewn across the window-benches
remains of a potluck on tables

the smell of pancakes
my mother's voice from outside
the candles she wears on her head

white dress billowing
now Helios has risen, Sunna ascends
their brightness in my yearning heart

Hello, Iris

2019.

Between sky and sea,
in the ozone scent after lightning
has descended, the freshness
following the patter of rain
coming down from above,
as impermanent as rainbows
after sky-shaking thunderstorms,
as deathless as light itself beaming,
in the places of reconciliation,
as stormy as our skies, you fly,
Iris, messenger of the Gods.
Remember — I was born under
your sign, the double rainbow
visible from my mother's
hospital bed that June day.
Remember — I worshipped you,
drawn to that symbol at first,
until the rainbow dissolved,
dissipated into light so fine,
and you dazzled me, shook me,
poured in a beauty so great
that all I could speak was praise.
When I wrote Enahari,
you were at her heart, Iris —
the Goddess of the thousand suns,
she who is radiant with color,
who brings governance,
her light purifying all,

the mother of Enakhiavoshei,
and your name was the core
embedded and transmitted
through the conlang —
ena, divine, *hari* meaningless
beyond bearing your spark.
Over a decade onward,
I have not uttered your name
at my shrine, have not given
incense that shimmers upward.
I forgot that *Enahari* was you
until what I wrote at sixteen
stared up at me and I gave the ink
to the rubbish pile, releasing
the teenage angst and prayers,
all fertilizer for joys to come soon.
Hello, Iris — what basic words.
A dip of incense into fire,
what an easy, practiced gesture.
Hello, Iris — you reconcile all,
a Goddess of conciliation,
negotiation, all skills to heal.
Hello, Iris — in a murmur,
I say it, repeat it, until my palms
find resolve to face up.

A Catalog of Doubts

2019.

each doubt I hold close
a box given at birth filled
released in dying

a box given at birth filled
cognition racing
questions sharp as cut diamonds

released in dying
if the soul is eternal
upon the meadow

what I wrote so young
fantasies with no substance
questioning judgments

fantasies with no substance
how can we believe
anything once we have strayed

questioning judgments
Parmenides' verses steady
nectar in my ears

from childhood, firmness
am I a waste, having none?
Sallust would say yes

am I a waste, having none?
rickety boats move
the endpoint is what matters

Sallust would say yes
foolishly taught, nothing more
no steadiness, no light

On a Bench in College

2019.

We sat near the fountain statue
remembering a girl who once was
a student, dead, a tragedy,
on the Smith College campus.
It was late — we were students —
and I asked her what she
thought about Gods,
the universe — perhaps selfish,
I wanted something reassuring,
an anchor from darkness
that filled me whenever my mind
expanded out to encompass
the totality of life and death,
when it betrayed me to show
our sun's far-future nova
destroying whatever remains
billions of years in the future;
she, an atheist, had nothing.
I have always harbored
more doubts about people
than about Gods, even then,
when eternity bewitched each blink,
the universe on my shoulders
invisible to her and to me.

Hermes, Giver of Joy

2011.

Think about your choices —
who will go with you down that hard road?
Some will share your burden,
others must leave in time to search after
fresh brains and smooth skin.
One will hold your hand,
the other will shrink away when rot
overcomes your limbs and your senses decay.
You want someone reliable
to hold that lantern and keep it burning —
a fennel-stalk shining in the darkness
as you make your way down.
And who better than someone who goes,
who comes, always wandering —
he at the outskirts of the city
where grass pokes through the sidewalk cracks,
he who plays in the tidal pools where ocean
meets beach, where beach meets grass,
where grass gives way to concrete and city?
Think about your choices, but don't choose —
at least, not too soon, not before wisdom
has taught you whom you may rely on.

TO KEEP THE LANTERN BURNING (RELIANCE)

2020.

Going back nine sharp years —
how to retrace paths now overgrown,
a single thread
        leading,
a labyrinth
        unfolding
with nothing at its cavernous center.

Clarity brings me home —
to know the self is not a single instant,
the upward trek
        opening,
each bramble
        waylaying,
both steps to the transient-blooming nectar.

I have pondered the way here —
each petition consecrated by dragon's blood,
candles once-lit
        shining,
these prayers
        illuminating
as the years wove a fragrant tapestry.

It was always about truth —
yet soon, as the cascade awakened deep,
newfound concerns

       flitting,
I sought
       grounding:
the knowledge that such good would not just leave.

Consider several drivers —
pragmatism and piety, fear and happiness,
from the intensity
       flinching
(my heart
       tightening
when I dreaded severed threads, a melody lost).

Reliance never comes
from unsteady wanderings and fanciful thoughts;
each of us
       grasping —
our callow hearts
       craving —
self-deceive, love and fear such untidy oceans.

Reliance may yet come,
no simple choice, but a pivot point bearing us —
all Gods steadfast
       pilots,
our own perspectives
       oscillating
these roads always taken, now taking, yet bare.

A Gift of Ink and Water

2018.

when I was so small Mnemosyne
presented a jar swirling with keys
tipped it against my waiting lips
said *drink* in a cavernous voice
like shooting stars falling
black as ink sucking into diary paper
the heat memory of the big bang
lightlessness beyond fires
warming generations with stories
nectar like drowning in passionfruit
coming to the bottom of a deep pool
glancing through telescopes
at the vastness that lies beyond
Saturn and Jupiter so crisp
with their torch-like moons
they almost don't seem real
recollections in rich color
emotions cascading as if present
and past had merged together
drawn down into a lake opaque
as unlit water in her jar

memory is like a good kitchen knife
necessary to cut through things
with skill and attention
dangerous when it slips out of control
hazard lurks in the dusty places
memory absorbs into its folds

poisons that swell it to bursting
the blade of memory is the strong tide
experience leaves in its wake
all those instants of rejection
hard knocks of kids whose voices
echo down through years like moldy
softness invading dried peppers
their moisture welling up through
one's eyes like fiery capsaicin
memories that notice howling voices
that even when justice moves them
cut into my heart like whirling glass

because memory opens up passively
impartial as patterns unlock it
dislodges total recall of emotions
sensations of being bullied
alongside the voices saying
you don't matter at all and why
are you so weak that words targeted
at people who do terrible things
plunge you underwater trapped
choking you with all those times
people did horrible things to you
and the loneliness of knowing
everyone would say it was your fault
your belief that everyone is out
for blood and that all failure
trains other people on your throat
all these fears backed up by memories
cataloged indexed organized by type

fill yourself with good things

those times you brought others happiness
every beautiful sentence whisked
from sages like foam on boiling beans
successes that make constellations
Mnemosyne always intended memory-ink
to swirl mesmerizingly like household
Gods shedding abundance in snakeskin
and poisons that do not kill bring
strength empathy kindness arete
let memory spill over with these
a Zeus Ktesios jar blessing you with
a harvest ripe with achievements
warm moments with friends and family
like heavy wool blankets and duvets
folded beautifully in storerooms

Mousai

2011.

Drenched in the light of the Mousai,
I wander through halls etched finely with words,
in stadiums crowded with voices,
hardly knowing myself over this noise.
The stories bubble up and flow out,
shining and twisting in the staccato light
of neurons firing until syllables
flow out like ichor ignited by strife.
They have hit me with their current.
Images erupt, so vivid, restless —
as if I am copper through which they run.
They are Orpheus, and I am the lyre
he brought to the underworld and back.
They have torn open my skull to root down,
coming into this still-callow body.
They twist me and turn me in their dance,
spinning us close to the sun where
Ikaros fell into the wine-dark sea.

Rediscovery

2019.

fragrant like smoke and heat
rising up from my skin
an incense of limbs
small stillness expanding
contracting
come to rest like swan
down tossed in breezes
eyes of your image
follow me across thresholds
a fire burns the color
of sharpness and marble
cold beneath
brushing fingertips
watched
my skin goes taut
as if it is dancing
you knot in through
that part of my brain
beyond thought
what does it mean
to be watched like this
licked by serpents
hands bound
hair free
intellect wide open

Fragments With No Homes

2019.

go to the oracle
ask the number of years
billions of candles, rivers of wax
she plucks pulsars from between her lips
like apples destined for the feast
they shimmer and scream like tree-roots
ripped up from so long ago
petrified splinters of life

I bind my hair with a robe like the sun

her lips hold screaming pulsars
shimmering, screaming like tree-roots
pulled up within the deep forest
they turn and they turn, we turn
we turn, our seconds fleeting,
the shapes we make stretching on,
moving out, pulling back in

poetry breaking like waves
a horizon the aftermath of chords
the silence of breath after the orchestra
stops, the conductor yet with hands lifted

I went to the mountains
where rock tastes bitter
drenched with sweet honey
I have heard the last words

the trees whispered before
the chasm opened below us

Julian's Ghost

Early 2010s, with some parts from 2019.

I.

Give me incense rising from ancient shrines;
make my prayers electrons that unlock
secrets in underground sanctuaries.
Cup my hands to greet the morning sun.
Let me rise immaculately from primordial seas.
Drop me from celestial debris, a stardust heroine.

Temples crumble, but actions remain forever,
crouching like a lover at the edge of dreaming.
She is mathematics and bruising winter wind,
self-born and eternally fertile, Universe herself.
Churches shackle her to a man from Galilee,
but she remains hidden in the naked sky.

II.

The feeling comes when I go
down the highway,
music on the radio.
One song will play.
Suddenly
high-speed wheels
nuclear war
buried saints
cities bursting —
all of it disappears.

I see you standing
in the window of some
Gallic house.
Troops wait below.
They cry. I weep.
Who you are catches me,
trapping me in the bottleneck's shaft.
I cannot breathe.
Fingers straining, I try to grasp you.
For a moment our eyes meet,
but when my hand touches
your cloak, you fall back
transparent as smoke and ash
and I am once again
this girl crying
over your broken body.

III.

years ago, decluttering
I found the baptismal cross,
its energy like a bruise on my fingertips.

when I read Vidal
the library book jacket rustled,
a fence through which I peeked at you.

the taurobolium, endless
purifications of the mind, body —
I see you and you see me, together reaching.

we are the people of charred
rosemary, fragments of salt dried
on the pathways to our shrines, scattered

like roses after the water dried.
my first thought on seeing it was you,
what it means when objects become pregnant

with meaning we do not value,
even when we do not remember, long
before we could utter words that mean consent.

INSPIRALING

2019.

with what words do I hymn you
when my tongue falls this still
as light descends like curtains
what symbols do I bear for you
but the snake that leaves its
traces in hot summer sand
what epithets remain after
words descend fatigued
from their syllabic dance
beyond sight beyond image
in this vastness serpentine
like summer flowers dancing
breath lingering at song's end
creak of a bow stretching taut
slippery as a dolphin's skin
transient as temple smoke

Eumenideia

2013.

When my arms stretched high,
they came from below, the ones
with snakes shimmering in their hair.

The heavens, the underworld,
and all spaces in the cracks of existence
teeming with the reality of Gods opened.

They filled the spaces within me
with the biting venom, pressing
snakes against my waiting lips.

To Womanly Herakles

2017.

Sometimes, it's the fourth day of the month
when the moon is still a pale sliver in the thumb
of blue day sky, but it's always Herakles who gets the
    incense
fired up and smoking from hissing lightning because the
    fourth day
means Aphrodite, Eros, Hermes, and this God
who some say was once a man, murdered by
women — unintentionally.
Sometimes, on the fourth day, when I light the incense
and read his hymns, I think, what am I doing here
because I am a feminist.

I once saw translations of the Orphic hymns online
that omitted him and Zeus both for their deeds.
Woman-Hater is one of Herakles' epithets.
and when I knew better, that Woman-Hater means
women could not be in his worship circles in some places,
lighting incense on the fourth day was honestly in the
    same
category as burying family infighting at a wedding:
Bare minimum, respectful, and disengaged,
a balance of honoring one another and self-preservation.
I still lit that incense because who am I to break the chains
    of tradition
when half of the point of this is rebuilding what was lost to
    fifteen hundred
years of some bureaucracy telling us we could not have

>   Goddesses
peeking out at us from temple alcoves.

And that's when I started digging into the deep earth,
a sacrifice of time and effort in the chthonic
realm where old and new scholarship meet and academics
>   tell stories.
It's never as simple as hate and love and I am old enough
>   to know.
Herakles is the God of marriage worshipped alongside
>   Hera and Hebe.
In most places women worshipped him, too.
On Kos Island, the priest dressed in women's clothes for
>   sacrifice
because Herakles has done that, manly-man that he is,
and bridegrooms decked out in women's adornments to
>   receive their brides.

It is never so easy, love and hate.
It varies from place to place, like states of our hearts.
What does it mean about us that we see how men behave
and how they take that story of Herakles' death to
>   demonize women
when some mythologies led to wedding rituals
and women worshipping this God freely.
Think about the narratives we teach ourselves
because it is never that simple and sometimes the answer
is somewhere between extreme points.
Patriarchy does so much, but one of those things is to make
>   us
see the bad things in people and Gods or say that
men cross-dressed as priests to protect Herakles from
>   women

or that his women priestesses needed to be virgins until
        death
as if virginity is a yoke that means anything more than that
she has said *fuck you* in the profane sense of the term to all
        men
in favor of being her own human in the audience of God.

Perhaps it is not so odd, then, to take my lightning-lighter
on the fourth day and intone hymns softly,
reclaiming this space that some men have said is theirs
and that real history reveals is not so clear cut.
Gods slip into the spaces that people open for them.
When I honor Herakles at my shrine,
let him come in his guise as a womanish man.

ON MYSTERIES AND BONDS

2019.

A chaste woman is given grace
within the mysteries of Dionysos —
not forced to drown down wine —
allowed to worship with her will
intact. One cannot always see scars.

Who knows which of us bear bruises
throbbing like Rhea's quick drumbeat
and for whom a mystery is learning
how to loosen one's grip on the
thyrsus. Not all need to be strung.

For us, all safety is a brutal
lesson won hard through prayer.
The mysteries rest in calm silence,
in warmth, in the goodness of Gods.
To mend takes more than to break.

ENTHRALLMENT

2017.

In asana, breath moves down my chest, a bellows
igniting a bright fire to course through my body.
The *Yoga Sutras* refined my understanding of this.
Vikalpaha is the imagination of metaphor, sleek,
and it is here where the great inferno blooms wide.
Asana prepares the body through movement to turn
inward and touch the deep-radiating light.
I think of those stone holders for tea lights
carved with stars, moons, and shooting meteors,
only in my mind's eye this is made of paper.
It is simultaneously yoga, the images on the cave
wall coming into focus, and the mirror held up
by the Titans to entrance Zagreus, whom they kill.
In asana, when I prepare my body and breathe deep,
I wonder if yoga is compatible with this imagined
world that I hold as an image against my mind's eye
because the fire that illumines it and brings it
into focus is the center of my being turned outward —
at this garden of delights that absorb my attention.
The vividness is so strong sometimes that I drown,
engrossed in light more deeply than I am in meditation.
Is this yoga, then, to move my body in preparation
for a work that I have sworn to Gods I will do,
for which I have given offerings of incense and time,
something that has brought me through highs and lows,
space to make theogony and mythology for Gods I love?
It is something like yoga, to prepare in asana,
to entrance oneself in images moving through the soul.

It is something like yoga, to breathe into this fire,
controlling it just enough to keep paper from curling.

HOUSE OF INK

2019.

Tonight, I thrash
in the chamber of ink.
She waits at its edge, crowned in seven,
black and red,
wet ink and dry papyrus,
smooth as a nib,
yielding as computer keys.
Through these foaming waters I come to her,
Seshat who lays out perimeters,
who has corralled
animals' shapes into human
voices bound in images.
Lady of the vultures
and the dogs,
holder of the sounds,
grinder of the ink,
help me move.
Grant me the endurance
to penetrate herein,
to swim through the sea
without hungering for its shore.

On Thargelia

2019.

For the first part,
I make an image —
myself not my self —
all I once wanted
unformed, malformed,
shaped from thought
lingering like gravel
grit and sooty snow.
From the air, I catch
echoes of words
ill-spoken, anxieties
I wove tight and fast,
a heritage acquired
from blood, the price
of being *here* at this
inflection point.

For the second, I fill
it with nothing
until it inflates out
enough like life to fool
those who do not see
breath or still minds.
It is time to lay this
all to rest in earth
where the structures
will uncoil themselves,
rotting into harmless

impressions of what was.
Pythios, take this, let
it fall away like the
one you slew at the navel.

For the final section,
I declare the foundations
into being, grounded firm,
open to light through which
stars fall like pinpricks,
seeing reduced to nothing
as if I am beyond this
tumultuous embrace of air.

Illuminated, so strange
to think the images
we made can still harm,
still bear stains that seep —
relentless — to weigh us down
saturated, even with no
share of deep-peaked
permanence that carries
up with the smoke,
up with the sound,
out and beyond,
circling and encircled
like twin stars dancing,
binary geometries
marking out the empty
fullness at their center,
your harmonies coloratura
pulsations that cleanse
even watching from afar.

Suspension

2019.

who watches the night, who keeps this lamplight
who keeps the winds from spitting flames to dissolution
in this world of changeability and confusion
I am pulled back into the heart of myself like strings
shocking expanses of air into note and overtone
this body like a focal point of pitted glass while still
behind my eyes the emanations refract and convex

this dance that self-revolves, that breathes itself,
this heart of a star so hot to touch even the thought
leaves my fingertips burning, my hand recoiling
while my lips taste the edges of honey that now
in my belly sings out like the oscillation of pulsars
you are a whisper and a knowing, a pathway worn
deep from the weaving of epithets through air

impermanence has taught me the sign of *brittle*
the delicate veins of mold that trace over dead leaves
a reflection of the honeycomb web we inhabit
the radials of gravity that sweep us together
that cluster matter tight into ember-like brilliance
and put out stellar nurseries like snuffed candles
these graveyards that seem so beautiful from afar

there is nothing impermanent in your brightness
the coiling matter I mistook for pollution loosens
the union within tips down and out like liquid light
an infinity of chords converges into soundless hum

I could reach into this vastness and torrent forth words
division and recombination and union as a pattern
the potential of sheet music, a breath before song

and yet it breaks against the shores of my body
this wholeness a sudden memory of falling deep
the honey a sticky aftertaste at the tip of my tongue
once again, I see the sign of *brittle*, yet it has no hold
your agalma's stare collides into me like photons
ionizing emission nebulae, your prayer beads so blue
I could fall again into a depth like eventide sky

About the Author

Kaye Boesme is a poet, conlanger, and writer. Her poetry has appeared in *Kaleidotrope*, *Illumen*, and *Eternal Haunted Summer*, and she has a short story in *The Society of Misfit Stories Presents*. More information about her publications and ongoing work is available at kayeboesme.com. She maintains a religious blog, *KALLISTI: Essays*, at kallisti.blog.

In her everyday life, Boesme works as an academic librarian. Her 2020 pandemic officemate is a sixteen-year-old cat named Yoyo. This is her first collection of poetry.

www.ingramcontent.com/pod-product-compliance
Lightning Source LLC
Chambersburg PA
CBHW032123090426
42743CB00007B/437